D0031324

A Friend
in the Storm

CHERYL RICKER

ZONDERVAN

A Friend in the Storm
Copyright © 2010 by Zondervan

Requests for information should be addressed to:

Zondervan, *Grand Rapids, Michigan 49530*

ISBN 978-0-310-51993-5

Design by Jody Langley

Printed in China

10 11 12 13 14 15 16 • 23 22 21 20 19 18 17 16 15 14 13 12 11 10 9 8 7 6 5 4 3 2

To:

_____

From:

_____

Date:

_____

No!!!

Struck by dread and endless questions
in the thick of instant night,
tears and fears consume me empty,
shred my grit to stick the fight.

Hands and lips uplift me briefly
but they miss my bleeding core;
Then the sound of Comfort whispers,
"I will show you something more …"

When filled with holy truth the mind rests.

....

– CHARLES SPURGEON

"Come to me, all you who are weary and burdened,

and I will give you rest."

....

MATTHEW 11:28

Step Together

In whirlwinds of confusion
when cold questions press you tight,
ask Me close and I will hold you
by a love surpassing sight.

You're My treasure, bright with promise,
and I live to see you reign;
As we cross this bridge together,
I will lead you through your pain.

X

Every step toward Christ kills a doubt.

....

– THEODORE CUYLER

"So do not fear, for I am with you ...
I will strengthen you and help you;
I will uphold you with my righteous right hand."

....

ISAIAH 41:10

Closer

My arm enfolds your shoulders
as I whisper sweet and warm;
Past the haze, into My rays,
we'll move in tune to beat this storm.

Though your eyes remain part-clouded
by your grief and shrouding fear,
heart-to-heart you'll start to see Me
through a lens that's growing clear.

God had one Son on earth without sin,
but never one without suffering.

....

— ST. AUGUSTINE

He was despised and rejected by men,
a man of sorrows, and familiar with suffering.

....

ISAIAH 53:3

Lifted

I let the path of suffering
rip and tear Me to the core;
The naked shame of all the world
upon My Spirit tore.

Rejected and despised,
I let them lift Me in your place;
So in your path of pain today,
be lifted free with grace.

God takes life's pieces and gives us unbroken peace.

....

– W.D. GOUGH

The LORD is close to the brokenhearted

and saves those who are crushed in spirit.

....

PSALM 34:18

Finisher

When it feels like life has failed you
and your mind's been cast in war,
please remember Love's forever;
I will pass you through this door.

You don't cry alone in battle,
even when you think you've lost.
Please believe this truth, My winner:
Heaven paid your victor cost.

The Almighty has his own purposes.

....

– ABRAHAM LINCOLN

The LORD your God is with you,
he is mighty to save.
He will take great delight in you,
he will quiet you with his love,
he will rejoice over you with singing.

....

ZEPHANIAH 3:17

You

You're forever on My mind
and in your presence I rejoice;
Singing out your name with angels,
all your sweetness fills My voice.

Keeping loved ones in My keeping,
I embrace a constant calm.
Whole and holy, I will hold you,
ever-after in My palm.

Worrying does not empty tomorrow of its sorrow –

it empties today of its strength.

....

– CORRIE TEN BOOM

"My peace I give you.

I do not give to you as the world gives.

Do not let your hearts be troubled

and do not be afraid."

....

JOHN 14:27

Peacescape

Receive My peace inside your eyes;
Though rivers rage, hope never dies.
I'll see you past the end of fear
'til gifts unfold like spring fresh cheer.

I'll spread your wings across the night;
With deepest peace, I'll give you sight …
to see beyond this purposed pause
into the light of My applause.

Travel or meditation, tranquilizers or therapy can bring
a measure of relief – but why settle for a mere reprieve
when God offers us real, genuine, personal peace.

....

– LUIS PALAU

Now may the Lord of peace himself give you
peace at all times and in every way.

....

2 THESSALONIANS 3:16

Higher

How I long to lift you higher
through this dose of close relief,
give new joy amidst this trial,
make great healing through your grief.

Knowing no one steals your feelings,
let regret and blaming cease;
Feet on mine, I'll lightly lead you
to this place of quiet peace.

Providence has at all times been my only dependence,
for all other resources seem to have failed us.

....

– GEORGE WASHINGTON

Do not be anxious about anything, but in everything,
by prayer and petition, with thanksgiving, present
your requests to God. And the peace of God, which
transcends all understanding, will guard your hearts
and your minds in Christ Jesus.

....

PHILIPPIANS 4:6-7

Counselor

My quiet place is open
every solitary day;
Waiting eagerly to see you,
open time is all you pay.

I'm by far a better listener
than this world's best-listening man;
If you're stuck on what to tell Me,
think again. I understand.

Our weakness should render us able to speak to God
with daring, for Love is vulnerable to weakness.

....

– PIERRE WOLF

Cast your cares on the LORD and he will sustain you.

....

PSALM 55:22

Rest

Throw Me all your passing worries,
pressing thoughts and testy weights,
past confusions, mass intrusions;
Throw Me all your human hates.

Letting go, you'll find true lightness
from the One who took your shame.
I'm a pro at trading burdens;
After all, that's why I came.

What a wonderful thing to know, to remember,
to remind yourself of when you feel overwhelmed with
busyness or with pain. You don't have to come to
him quiet. You just need to come to him.

....

– EMILIE BARNES

I pour out my complaint before him;
before him I tell my trouble.

....

PSALM 142:2

Why?

Why would a God who loves so strong
allow this blow of senseless wrong
enwrap me in this shock of pain
that tries to snuff what's kept me sane?

With failing strength, I'm struck down low,
so where's this peace supposed to flow?
Inside this hole where dreaming dies
beneath bare groans and screaming cries?

God does not send despair in order to kill us;

he sends it in order to awaken us to new life.

....

– HERMAN HESSE

Jesus wept. Then the Jews said,

"See how he loved him!"

....

JOHN 11:35-36

Lazarus

I knew he'd die without Me
but I tarried extra days;
For My bigger-picture purposes,
I'd turn their grief to praise.

For an instant I'd weep with them,
fellow-foe of pain and death;
Shouting life and strength back to him,
hope awoke with heaven's breath.

Our Lord has written the promise of resurrection, not in books alone, but in every leaf in springtime.

. . . .

– MARTIN LUTHER

Jesus said, "I am the resurrection and the life."

. . . .

JOHN 11:25

Bouquet

When fear-fierce pain saps energy
and wilts your hopeful thoughts,
from bended knee, I'll let you see
My sweet forget-me-nots.

My Word's an open flower,
fragrant, healing, blooming gift;
When I say, "I'm yours forever,"
rest in truth and take a whiff.

As the flower turns to the sun, or the
dog to his master, so the soul turns to God.

....

– WILLIAM TEMPLE

"To him who is thirsty, I will give to drink without cost
from the spring of the water of life."

....

REVELATION 21:6

Living Word

Come thirsty to My brook of hope
and you won't leave Me dry.
I do what no mere man can do;
I fully satisfy.

My water's pure and holy
as it sloshes through your soul;
Come sip My living power
as I resurrect you whole.

There is strength …

There is peace …

There is hope …

There is power …

There is life in the voice that sounds

like rushing water.

....

– ANNE GRAHAM LOTZ

"My sheep listen to my voice;

I know them, and they follow me."

....

JOHN 10:27

Heaven's Breeze

As you gaze through pain's wide window
feeling sliced by life's divide,
please remember Love's forever;
I won't ever leave your side.

Heaven's breeze whisks this warm whisper.
Listen close; I call your name.
When you whisper back, "My Father,"
you'll be better than the same.

Mastered by Christ, you can handle anything.

....

– RICK WARREN

A righteous man may have many troubles,

but the LORD delivers him from them all.

....

PSALM 34:19

Your Advocate

Don't worry when they judge you;
Only I can judge a heart.
As the Christ who crossed each crisis,
I will barricade each dart.

They misjudged Me for a devil,
peering gravely through pinched eyes,
but I gave beyond the grave
so I could save and make you wise.

God voluntarily put himself in the position of being
affected by creation. Love involves giving, and God,
self-complete, has only himself to give.

....

– PHILIP YANCEY

For this is what the LORD says:
"As a mother comforts her child,
so will I comfort you."

....

ISAIAH 66:13

In June

When you call Me, I will answer;
I will calm you to the quick.
I feel deep inside each flattening ache
that leaves your insides sick.

Since I made you in My power,
not one cell, synapse or nerve,
not one groaning of your spirit
ever passes Me unheard.

Troubles are often the tools by which
God fashions us for better things.

....

– HENRY WARD BEECHER

"See, I am doing a new thing!
Now it springs up; do you not perceive it?
I am making a way in the desert
and streams in the wasteland."

....

ISAIAH 43:19

Unwasted

When darkness stalks and skulks your brain
and clasps you in its cloak of pain,
breathe deep this truth that stills your soul:
I long prevail to make you whole.

I never waste a pang of pain,
a drip of tear or spot of stain.
My comfort pours new life in you,
in perfect time for others too.

First keep the peace within yourself,

then you can also bring peace to others.

....

– THOMAS A KEMPIS

He comforts us in all our troubles, so that we can

comfort those in any trouble with the comfort we

ourselves have received from God.

....

2 CORINTHIANS 1:4

Dance of Comfort

Just as My arm sweeps over yours,
My strength in you, to others, pours.
My truth in you now long declares,
your love loves stronger while it shares …

A prayer, a touch, a simple smile
reveals My Presence every mile.
There's always something you can do,
when prayer makes waves ahead of you.

The perseverance of the saints consists

in ever new beginnings.

....

– ALEXANDER WHYTE

"For I know the plans I have for you," declares the
LORD, "plans to prosper you and not to harm you,
plans to give you hope and a future."

....

JEREMIAH 29:11

Artisan

Poked inside this wind-licked fire
like a piece of molten glass,
letting prods and pliers take you
in for yet another pass …

Your smoked-color bends to beauty
'til you're clearly made My vase,
held together most transparent,
showing off, through you, My face.

Faith is the sight of the inward eye.

....

– ALEXANDER MACLAREN

In this you greatly rejoice, though now for a little while
you may have had to suffer grief in all kinds of trials.
These have come so that your faith—of greater worth
than gold, which perishes even though refined by fire—
may be proved genuine and may result in praise, glory
and honor when Jesus Christ is revealed.

....

1 PETER 1:6-7

Insight

True faith is never lame or blind;
It's sight deep-seen by souls.
Though eyes may take in rays of light,
they're still just two black holes.

The soul that sees Me sees
inside My Spirit-led dimensions;
The evidence of brand-new lives
reveals unseen connections.

If the works of God were such as might easily be comprehended by human reason, they could not be called wonderful or unspeakable.

....

– THOMAS A KEMPIS

The heavens declare the glory of God;
the skies proclaim the work of his hands.

....

PSALM 19:1

Nature's Song

Who can gaze at glistening rivers
under purple perfect skies
and deny these gifts were given
by a God all-true and wise?

I design to show My glory,
gleaming hints of majesty.
Come the day I blow back blackness,
clouded eyes, at last, will see.

People travel to wonder at the height of the mountains, at the huge waves of the seas, at the long course of the rivers, at the vast compass of the ocean, at the circular motion of the stars, and yet they pass by themselves without wondering.

....

– ST. AUGUSTINE

For all have sinned and fall short of the glory of God.

....

ROMANS 3:23

Choice

Sin slithered in the garden
with a choice to disobey,
plunging flesh inside its ruin,
binding life to blind decay ...

But I chose to die and save you,
break the curse and take the nails.
Glory rose through righteous suffering;
You were born through My travails.

God paints in many colors, but he never paints so gorgeously as when he paints in white.

. . . .

– G. K. CHESTERTON

"Come now, let us reason together,"
says the LORD.
"Though your sins are like scarlet,
they shall be as white as snow."

. . . .

ISAIAH 1:18

Foresight

Forming life-blood at creation,
I laid down your life's foundation.
As the Cornerstone, I waited
for My grace to be instated.

Scorning shame and Satan's bite,
I learned to crush him more each fight.
Cup of death in trembling hand,
I drank to you, a love long-planned.

To live by the law of Christ and accept him in our
hearts is to turn a giant floodlight of hope
into our valleys of trouble.

....

– CHARLES R. HEMBREE

For our light and momentary troubles are achieving for
us an eternal glory that far outweighs them all.

....

2 CORINTHIANS 4:17

Seedling

I brought you here to teach you love
displayed in growing trust;
As you tiptoe in My pathway,
I breathe breakthrough hope in dust.

Since I'm shaping you for heaven,
I rain comfort through your loss,
steady patience through your grappling,
true compassion through your cross.

The Christian life is a life of paradoxes. We must give to receive, realize we are blind to see, become simple to be wise, suffer for gain, and die to live.

....

– ANONYMOUS

"For my thoughts are not your thoughts,
neither are your ways my ways,"
declares the LORD.
"As the heavens are higher than the earth,
so are my ways higher than your ways
and my thoughts than your thoughts."

....

ISAIAH 55:8-9

Mystery

Sometimes this life makes little sense
to finite human brains
on their constant quest for answers
far outside of heaven's plains …

But if mere dust caught every clue
there'd be no room to trust,
and faith would lose its mystery,
eternity's brief must.

He who has no vision of eternity will
never get a true hold of time.

....

– THOMAS CARLYLE

We know that the whole creation has been groaning as
in the pains of childbirth right up to the present time.
Not only so, but we ourselves, who have the first fruits
of the Spirit, groan inwardly as we wait eagerly for our
adoption as sons, the redemption of our bodies.

....

ROMANS 8:22-23

Expecting

Life's contractions press you closer
past the door of time's tight tomb;
Stuck inside this world of testing,
you're still safe-sealed in My womb.

As My Spirit flows inside you,
guaranteeing your reward,
I will grow you, Child of value,
'til the day I cut the cord.

The distinction between past, present, and future is only an illusion, even if a stubborn one.

....

– ALBERT EINSTEIN

But do not forget this one thing, dear friends: With the Lord a day is like a thousand years, and a thousand years are like a day.

....

2 PETER 3:8

On Time

I hold you in My hourglass,
a chosen grain of sand.
Upside down or right-side up,
you move fast-forward like I planned.

Time is just a pressed-in moment,
just a narrow open door,
made to pass you into splendor
that awaits you on My shore.

The peace of God is that eternal calm which lies far
too deep in the praying, trusting soul to be reached by
any external disturbances.

....

– A.T. PIERSON

Trust in the LORD with all your heart
and lean not on your own understanding;
in all your ways acknowledge him,
and he will make your paths straight.

....

PROVERBS 3:5-6

Undying Hope

Hope reaches past your circumstance
when vaporous life is flawed.
In My plan, hope stands for certainty:
eternity with God.

Resting in My hand completely,
as the One who paid your cost,
I become your true direction
in a hope that's never lost.

Hope is not based upon denying reality but rather
upon affirming God's sovereignty.

....

— BILL KEMP AND DIANE KERNER ARNETT

Your eyes saw my unformed body.
All the days ordained for me
were written in your book
before one of them came to be.

....

PSALM 139:16

Sound Reason

Who can stand not understanding
all the blanks upon life's page?
Who can gaze at death undaunted
by its tempermental rage?

Who can feel Love's comfort singing
when a silent fit won't flee?
Who knows fist-sized brains are weak
because they're shaped to lean on Me.

When circumstances seem impossible, when all signs of grace in you seem at their lowest ebb, when temptation is fiercest, when love and joy and hope seem well nigh extinguished in your heart, then rest, without feeling and without emotion, in the Father's faithfulness ...

....

– D. TRYON

For I am convinced that neither death nor life, neither angels nor demons, neither the present nor the future, nor any powers, neither height nor depth, nor anything else in all creation, will be able to separate us from the love of God that is in Christ Jesus our Lord.

....

ROMANS 8:38-39

Beside My Cross

As he hung beside me guilty,
twisting gasps in choking thickness,
I dripped blood that spoke forgiveness
for each soul seeped in sin's sickness.

Seeing sin beside perfection,
he grasped one last pleading cry.
"Yes," I said, "you'll see My Kingdom.
No, your soul will never die."

I was enabled to go on because I had the word of a
perfect Gentleman, never known to break a promise,
that He would be with me always.

....

– DAVID LIVINGSTONE

"When you pass through the waters,
I will be with you."

....

ISAIAH 43:2

Hold On

There's always always always hope.
Just reach for Me, your safety rope.
When storms assail you, trust you'll float,
for by My strength, I'll help you cope.

The rope thrown off the boat for you
is never frayed. I'll see you through.
In Me, old hope is made brand new.
Hope longs to stay attached to you.

God never wastes pain. He always uses it to
accomplish His purpose. And His purpose is
for His glory and our good. Therefore, we can
trust Him when our hearts are aching or
our bodies are racked with pain.

....

– JERRY BRIDGES

Love always protects, always trusts,
always hopes, always perseveres.

....

1 CORINTHIANS 13:7

Invisible Places

I'm fixed on inner beauty
as I shoulder all your fears;
You don't weary Me with worry
when you pour it in My ears.

If you grasped how much I love you,
Child, you'd blush and even weep;
In My hand you're held like promises
of truth I'll always keep.

No man is able of himself to grasp the supreme good of eternal life; he needs divine help. Hence there is here a two-fold object, the eternal life we hoped for, and the divine help we hope by.

....

– ST. THOMAS AQUINAS

"I do believe; help me overcome my unbelief!"

....

MARK 9:24

Rhythmic Footsteps

Faith ebbs and flows, but never goes;
It grows a lifetime through.
It shows My win beside your sin
that I forget for you.

It works with grace that blots out shame
that lightens like a song;
When your life is at its bleakest,
in your weakness, I'll be strong.

God works by contraries so that a man feels
himself to be lost in the very moment when
he is on the point of being saved.

....

– MARTIN LUTHER

Look to the LORD and his strength;
seek his face always.

....

PSALM 105:4

Becoming

My face, though yet unseen,
grows ever clearer through this trial;
As the One who bore sin's imprint
in your place, I'll see you smile.

Healing peace from covered sin
sweeps sweetly in to lift your eyes,
to the One your life's reflecting
in the light of heaven's prize.

Healing in the Bible is not becoming what we were,
but becoming all that God intends us to be.

....

— RAY PRITCHARD

Heal me, O LORD, and I will be healed.

....

JEREMIAH 17:14

Healing

My heart is hard as ice, Lord;

Will you melt it with Your rain?

Dream new dreams inside my dreamer

'til my fears and tears can drain …

Upon my face, a trickling stream,

will healing waters pour?

Where ice left holes inside me,

will You fill me to the core?

In healing one can concentrate on either of two
attributes: the power of God or the love of God.
In every healing there is a manifestation of both.

....

– FRANCIS MACNUTT

"Be still, and know that I am God."

....

PSALM 46:10

You?

Will you love me back and hold Me?
Will you trust Me with your pain?
As the One who lifts the lowly,
will you let Me be your rain?

As you ask Me worthy questions,
do you hunger for My way?
As your true and healing Answer,
will I have your final say?

We are God's own—to Him, therefore, let us live and die. We are God's own; therefore let His wisdom and will dominate all our actions. We are God's own; therefore let every part of our existence be directed towards Him as our only legitimate goal.

....

– JOHN CALVIN

"Not my will, but yours be done."

....

LUKE 22:42

Humbly

I cried out in my waiting room
for hope to wake me up.
Abased, I paced in wonder,
"When would grace replace my cup?"

In a moment I stopped trying
as I lay there, calm and still.
That's the day I finally found Him,
waiting for my dying will.

Love is the greatest thing that God can give us;

for himself is love: and it is the greatest thing

we can give to God.

....

– JEREMY TAYLOR

To all who received him, to those who believed in his

name, he gave the right to become children of God.

....

JOHN 1:12

Heavenly Assurance

Lord of Love, I ask for cleansing
by Your blood that washes free.
Weak and broken, I will trust You;
Moving closer now, I see.

As your own, I pledge to serve You
with each breath of life You give.
Breathing in Your peace forever,
graced by faith in You, I'll live.

The glory of Christianity is to conquer by forgiveness.

....

– WILLIAM BLAKE

If we confess our sins, he is faithful

and just and will forgive us our sins and

purify us from all unrighteousness.

....

1 JOHN 1:9

Jubilation!

My dancing angels celebrate
before My glowing face,
laughing freely, you've been rescued;
I secured your resting place.

It's a lasting breeze of happiness;
You're safe and sound with Me;
Friend, you're all I've ever wanted;
I'm your lifetime Guarantee.

God's love is like a river springing up in the divine

substance and flowing endlessly through his creation,

filling all things with life and goodness and strength.

....

– THOMAS MERTON

There is a river whose streams make glad the city

of God, the holy place where the Most High dwells.

God is within her, she will not fall;

God will help her at break of day.

....

PSALM 46:4-5

Steady Now

Swinging high and low beside you,
I've become your steady beat;
Loving those you love still deeper,
I lead everybody's feet.

Others leave, but I stay fastened
like a waltz that knows no end.
In the midst of this, be light
because you're right with your Best Friend.

When Jesus takes your hand, He keeps you tight.
When Jesus keeps you tight, He leads you through
your whole life. When Jesus leads you through your
life, He brings you safely home.

....

— CORRIE TEN BOOM

"The LORD is my strength and my song;
he has become my salvation."

....

EXODUS 15:2

Heaven Inside

You waltzed inside my lonely room
and snuffed out doubt's unwelcome gloom.
Beyond these window panes I see
a glimpse of wide eternity.

Beyond my flesh that aches to grasp
Your healing truth, my soul, You clasp;
All thanks to love, You found my start;
The sound of home awakes my heart.

Acceptance is not resignation, giving up ...
Acceptance is active cooperation with God,
and it always includes gratitude.

....

– WARREN W. WIERSBE

He put a new song in my mouth,
a hymn of praise to our God.

....

PSALM 40:3

Sweet Dreams

When the night is long I'll praise You,
raising prayers against the storm,
letting truth direct my thinking,
breezing peace through my weak form.

Safe inside Your Spirit's blanket,
wiping tears like mourning dew,
I will whisper in the shadows,
"Lord, I'm still in love with You."

We can only appreciate the miracle of a sunrise if we
have waited in the darkness.

....

– UNKNOWN

In that day they will say,
"Surely this is our God;
we trusted in him, and he saved us.
This is the LORD, we trusted in him;
let us rejoice and be glad in his salvation."

....

ISAIAH 25:9

Freedom!

Your fight with pain will fall like chains
and never be remembered,
but love and joy will multiply
My perfect plan, unhampered.

Like Me, you'll fill with song
that wraps your mind in deepest peace;
Exploring free, forgetting grief,
you'll find your soul's release.

Joy is the serious business of heaven.

....

– C.S. LEWIS

No eye has seen, no ear has heard,
no mind has conceived what God has
prepared for those who love him.

....

1 CORINTHIANS 2:9

Bliss

A cacophony of colors,
brand new senses burst ignited;
Swinging, singing, laughing, clapping,
every moment, most delighted.

With a merry host of angels
in a revelry of flight;
Here and there, as free as air,
you'll see it all in brand-new light.

When we've been there ten thousand years,

bright shining as the sun,

we've no less days to sing God's praise

than when we first begun.

....

– JOHN NEWTON

And so we will be with the Lord forever.

....

I THESSALONIANS 4:17

Complete

Transparent streets of gleaming gold
and friends for endless miles …
You're dancing dreams of sheer delight;
Hugs greet you wide as smiles.

My love flows waves right through you,
bathing you in Glory's morn …
By fragrant gardens' endless blooms,
you're finally fully born.